The
Deerslayer

by James Fenimore Cooper

Abridged and adapted by T. Ernesto Bethancourt

Illustrated by James McConnell

A PACEMAKER CLASSIC

GLOBE FEARON
Pearson Learning Group

Other Pacemaker Classics

ISBN 0-8224-9285-7
Printed in the United States of America

7 8 9 10 11   08 07 06 05 04

Pearson Learning Group

1-800-321-3106
www.pearsonlearning.com

Contents

Introduction

The Deerslayer was written by James Fenimore Cooper more than 140 years ago. It is one of the most popular novels about American frontier life ever published.

The Deerslayer tells the story of a young man named Natty Bumppo. He and a fellow traveler named Harry March arrive in upstate New York in the 1740s. The book tells about the adventures of both men, their battles with unfriendly Indians, and their involvement with white settlers in the Otsego Lake country.

The Deerslayer is the first of Cooper's five novels which make up *The Leatherstocking Tales*. All five books are about Natty Bumppo. They follow his adventures from when he is a young man up until his old age. Of the other four, *The Last of the Mohicans* is probably the best-known.

The five stories in *The Leatherstocking Tales* show two different views of frontier life in the 18th century. Natty Bumppo and his Indian friends live a free life and show a strong concern for nature. The settlers helped to civilize the frontier. But at times they were careless in their treatment of the unspoiled wilderness.

James Fenimore Cooper was born in a small New Jersey town in 1789. He was raised in upstate New York in Cooperstown, a community that had been named for his father William. The beautiful countryside surrounding Cooperstown is the setting for *The Deerslayer*.

The author spent years writing about 18th century life in America. In addition to his frontier novels, James Fenimore Cooper wrote several exciting tales of the sea and stories about the American Revolution.

1 Going to Glimmerglass

One beautiful summer day in 1740, two young men were making their way through the forest that covered the state of New York in those times. They had met on the trail and had joined together, to better defend themselves from Indian attack.

For in those days, New York State was hardly settled. New York City was already old, but upstate was still ruled by a number of tribes of Native Americans. This isn't to say that all the red men were united against all white men. The Mingos were friendly to the French in Canada. They thought of the British as their enemies. The Mohicans were friendly to the British. They hated the French and Mingos.

But though different tribes owned different lands, there were no signposts in the forest. One found out that a place was unfriendly upon being attacked. And it was for this reason our two young men traveled together.

To look at them, one wouldn't think either man needed help. One man was a giant: six feet four inches tall and over two hundred pounds. His name was Harry March, though the Indians had named him "Hurry Harry." He was quick to laugh and quick to lose his temper. He wore clothing popular with white men of the time: knee-length pants, leather stockings, and a heavy coat over a rough linen shirt. It was obvious that Hurry Harry didn't care what he looked like. His clothes were messy and uncared for. But he carried a long rifle that was well cared for indeed.

The other young man couldn't have been more different from Hurry Harry. He was younger, about 24 to Harry's 28. He was just six feet tall, thin, and dressed all in buckskin leather, much like an Indian. In fact, he moved through the woods as silently as any Indian. This was hardly surprising, for he had been raised among the Mohican tribe, who had named him "Deerslayer."

Hurry Harry had killed a female deer, which he carried on his shoulder as though it were a feather. When the two men reached a clearing, Harry threw the animal to the ground and soon had a fire going. He cut a great slab of meat from the deer and held it over the fire just long enough to warm it.

"Have some, Deerslayer," Harry said, with a full mouth. "Show me that you've got a Mohican belly, as well as a Mohican education. Come, boy. Show your manhood. Or have they named you Deerslayer for nothing?"

"Not much manhood in killing a doe, Harry," said Deerslayer.

"Not much manhood in the Mohicans, either," said Harry. "Look at what the Mingos do to them. They steal their land, even their women. And what do the Mohicans do? Nothing, that's what!"

"Is it so wrong to want to live in peace?" asked Deerslayer. "The Mingos have broken treaties and filled the woods with their lies. But I've lived ten years with the Mohicans. They are as proud and manly as any tribe you can find."

"Well, to my mind, no red man's worth his salt," Harry said. "It's their nature. Especially when it comes to a fight. They're all cowards at heart. And I've got the scalps to prove it."

Deerslayer didn't say anything. He didn't know Harry well enough to speak his mind about white men taking scalps from fallen enemies. But he did know that the British would pay any white man a great deal of money for a scalp.

"And what about you, boy?" asked Harry. "How many scalps have you got?"

"None," said Deerslayer.

"You don't take scalps? You're losing money, boy."

"You don't understand me," said Deerslayer. "I mean I have never killed a man, red or white."

Hurry Harry roared with laughter. "Some man of the woods you are!" he said. "Well, no matter, boy. You'll get your chance. These woods are full of Mingos. They just came back from raiding your Mohican friends."

Deerslayer nodded. "I know. That's part of what brings me here." Then he said no more. He didn't like this big, coarse man. And the fact was, Deerslayer was on a mission. Somewhere, near Lake Otsego, or Glimmerglass as white men called it, he was to meet a friend. His friend was Chingachgook, a chief of the Mohicans.

Chingachgook's wife, Hist, had been stolen by the Mingos' raiding party. It would never have happened unless the Mingos had help. One of the Mohicans, Yocommon, had turned traitor. He wanted Hist for himself. When the Mohicans were away hunting, he led the Mingos to their camp, and Hist was stolen.

The men finished their meal and were soon on their way. After a short time, Harry pointed and said, "There she is . . . Glimmerglass."

Lake Otsego was as beautiful then as it is today. Its surface did indeed seem smooth as glass. On the eastern shore was a large log structure. It looked more like a fort than a cabin. "That's where we're going," Harry said. "And a fine welcome we'll get from Tom Hutter and his daughters."

"A white man with daughters out here?" asked Deerslayer. "A bit dangerous for women, isn't it?"

"You don't know Tom Hutter," Harry said. "That log castle yonder is safe as a church. See how it's on the edge of the lake? You can get to it only by water. No Indian could get over those walls that face the woods.

"And then Tom's got the ark. Great big flatboat, big as a house. He takes the ark and sees to his traps all along the lakeshore. He and his daughters live in the ark as much as they do the castle."

"Sort of like living on a ship," Deerslayer said.

"There you have it," said Harry. "Old Tom was a sailor once. Some folks say he was even a pirate with Captain Kidd. I know he's got a big old chest he keeps his treasures in. But to me, the biggest treasure he's got is his daughter Judith. She's going to marry me."

"Then you're engaged to her?"

"Not exactly," Harry said. "But I have an understanding with Old Tom. It's Judith that's the trouble. Oh, she's beautiful as a sunrise, she is. But she's flighty. Every now and then, the British soldiers come by. I think she likes Captain Warley. Him and his fancy ways and manners. If he goes near her, I'll kill him!"

"Seems to me the lady has a mind of her own," Deerslayer said. "And as you're not *really* engaged . . ."

Harry moved like a cat. In a second, he had Deerslayer by the throat. His face was inches from Deerslayer's as he said, "Any man that looks on Judith is a dead man. And that means you, too. Just remember that."

Deerslayer looked Harry right in the eye. If the big man thought to frighten Deerslayer, it didn't work. "I have no need for a wife," he said evenly. "My life is here in the woods. I live by my rifle. There is no woman who wants a life like mine. And I would never ask a woman to share it."

Harry relaxed his grip. "Just as well," he said. Then his dark mood passed. He smiled and said, "Sorry, boy. It's just that when it comes to Judith, I get crazy sometimes. No harm meant. But let's go. Tonight we'll have venison, made by Judith and her sister, Hetty. Oh, don't mind Hetty, boy. She's kind of plain. And she's not quite right in the head . . . a bit slow, if you know what I mean."

"That won't bother me," Deerslayer said. "The Mohicans, like all Indians, respect folks that are slow in the mind. They think it's a sign that their god has touched a person."

"Indian god?" Harry snorted. "They don't have gods. They're savages, that's all. But come on, our journey's end is in sight!"

2 Deerslayer Meets the Hutters

The meal was not to be. When the two men arrived, the log castle was empty. "Old Tom is out on the lake someplace," said Hurry Harry. He looked through Tom Hutter's things and found an old telescope. "Ah, just as I thought," Harry said, using the glass. "He's at the far end of the lake. I can see the ark."

"Are they returning?" asked Deerslayer.

"No. We must go to them," Harry replied. "I know where Tom has hidden some canoes. Come with me."

In a short time, the two men were paddling toward the far end of the lake. As they did, Harry kept up his talk about red men being less than human. Deerslayer stayed silent. Minutes later, their canoe entered a small cove. The ark drifted lazily near the edge of the water. As the canoe approached the shore, the overgrown bushes brushed against the two men's heads.

"There he is," Harry said. "I can see Old Tom. He's up to his knees in mud, checking his traps. But I'll bet you Judith isn't helping him at all. Most likely she's doing her hair at the lakeshore, where she can see her own pretty face."

"I think you're too hard on her, Harry," Deerslayer said. "Women work just as hard as men do. And if her father works out in the mud, chances are she helps him at home . . . cleaning or preparing a meal."

Suddenly the bushes parted. Deerslayer grabbed for his rifle, and then he stopped. He was face to face with a beautiful young woman, only inches away!

"How good it is to hear the truth from a man's lips," she said. "And as for you, Harry, anything kind would stick in your throat." The lovely young woman smiled at Deerslayer. "But at least you're keeping better company these days."

It was with these words that Deerslayer first met Judith Hutter. Harry had not lied about Judith's beauty, Deerslayer noted.

Within moments, the two men pulled right alongside the ark. Soon they were on board the big flatboat.

At the far end of the boat sat another young woman. She was doing some needlework. As Deerslayer came near her, she looked up.

"You are Hetty Hutter," Deerslayer said. "Harry has told me about you."

"Yes, I am," said the girl. "And what is your name?"

"I have many names," Deerslayer said. "Some were given to me by my family, others by the Mohicans."

"Then tell me *all* your names," said the girl, with a sweet smile. "And I will tell you what I will think of you."

"I was named for my father . . . Nathaniel. Or Natty, if you will. My last name is Bumppo."

"How nice," said the girl. "I am Hetty, and you are Natty. You are Bumppo, and I am Hutter. But Bumppo isn't as pretty a name as Hutter, is it?"

"It isn't fancy, I admit. But a whole lot of us have gone bumping through life with it. Besides, I don't go by that name. I go by what the Mohicans call me. And among them, I have several names."

"Oh, do tell me those, too," said Hetty. Deerslayer could see that the girl thought this was all a game. Harry had told the truth about Hetty and her mind.

"Well," said Deerslayer, "when I first was among the Indians, they called me 'Straight-tongue,' because they found out I never lied."

"Now, that is a good name. What else do they call you?"

"Once I got my rifle, they found out I could bring home enough venison to feed a family," said Deerslayer. "Then they began to call me what I go by now: Deerslayer. It's a name of honor. You see, the Mohicans prize a man who can feed people— not a man who can kill people."

"How right they are!" cried Hetty. "But my sister doesn't think that way. She likes the soldiers that come to see us now and then. She thinks they look handsome in their bright coats. But I know better. Their business is killing people. I hate them. And because you are a man of peace, I shall like you very much, Natty."

Just then, Old Tom Hutter came aboard, and he was greeted loudly by Hurry Harry. "I looked for you last week," said Tom. "What happened to you? And who is this you have brought with you?"

Harry explained how he and Deerslayer met on the trail. Old Tom took Deerslayer's hand and shook it. But there was little trust in the old man's eyes. "You dress like an Indian, boy," he said.

Deerslayer explained his manner of dress to Hutter. The old man nodded. "Well, if you're with the Mohicans, you're in trouble, boy. The old wars with the Mingos are starting up again. And they're out there in the woods. Look at what I found near my traps."

He showed Deerslayer a water-soaked moccasin. "That's Mingo, all right," said Deerslayer. "From

way up north, near Canada. But I don't think this came from any war party."

"What makes you say that?" asked Tom.

"If an Indian on the warpath lost a moccasin, he'd look for it until he found it. Otherwise, people would know he had been there. No, I think it was some Mingo out hunting."

"By Ned," the old man said, "you do know your redskins, don't you." He put out his hand again and shook Deerslayer's. This time there was true warmth in the handshake. "Glad to have you aboard the ark, lad. You'll be of help."

The old man began to untie the ropes that held the ark to the shore. Harry and Deerslayer helped him. "Don't relax too much, Mr. Hutter," Deerslayer said. "I have also seen signs of Mingos as we traveled here. They are all around us."

"How come you didn't tell me what you saw?" demanded Hurry Harry.

"It wouldn't have meant much to you," Deerslayer said. "A twig snapped here, a blade of grass broken. Mingos use them like signs in the forest. You have to know what to look for."

The men finished loosening the ropes. Tom took a long pole and pushed it against the shore. The great flatboat began to move out onto the lake. Something in the low-hanging trees caught Deerslayer's eye. He grabbed at his rifle and cried out to Harry. "Quick! Help Tom get us moving!"

Suddenly, a war party of six Indians began firing rifles and arrows from their hiding places in the trees. The flatboat passed, and several red men tried to jump onto the barge. But it was too late. Harry, with the strength of his great frame, was poling for all his worth. The Mingos fell into the water, and the ark floated freely onto the waters of Glimmerglass.

3 Le Loup Cervier Names Hawkeye

It was getting dark as the ark glided out onto Glimmerglass. Harry and Old Tom were laughing. Each congratulated the other on his part in driving off the Mingos.

"We were lucky, that's all," Deerslayer told them. "They had no canoes and couldn't follow us."

"You're right, lad," said Old Tom, getting serious. "We must get busy now. I have two canoes hidden along the lakeshore. We have to get them, before the Mingos find them."

Soon they were poling the ark near the shore. They quickly found one canoe. Just as they were nearing the second one, Harry grabbed at Deerslayer's arm. "Look over there," he said, pointing toward the woods farther down the shore. "Campfires! The Mingos are over there."

"There are no braves there," said Deerslayer. "Braves on the warpath wouldn't show where they were. That is their home camp. You'll find no one there but women and children. The Mingos often travel with their families."

"All the better!" cried Hurry Harry. "Let's find the other canoe. This is our chance to get rich!"

"I don't understand," said Deerslayer.

"I do," said Tom. "With only women and children there, we can raid the camp. There'll be enough scalp money for us all!"

Deerslayer said nothing. Soon they had found the other canoe, and they tied it up behind the ark. Then they poled the ark along the shore toward the Indians' camp. Harry and Tom loaded their rifles, and each man took a pistol. "Well, will you come with us?" Harry asked Deerslayer.

"I will come with you, but only to guard the canoes," Deerslayer said. "If something goes wrong, you will lose more than your lives. The Mingos will get your canoes, and then they will come after Hetty and Judith here on the ark.

"As for the scalps, I can be silent no longer. First, I will not make war on women and children. Second, I do not believe white men should take scalps. It's different for the red man. It's part of his religion. But for a white man, taking a scalp is a sin. I'm a poor Christian at best, but I feel that taking scalps is against the word of our God."

"Well, there's no sin in getting rich, is there?" asked Harry, laughing. "Or maybe you're just not up to killing a man, is that it?"

"In honest warfare, you'll not find me lacking," said Deerslayer. "But I will not kill women and children."

"Suit yourself," said Harry, as he got into a canoe. Deerslayer got into the other canoe and followed them. Soon they were approaching the shore, near the light of the Mingo campfires.

Tom threw a rope to Deerslayer, who knew what was needed of him. Once the other men went ashore, if anything went wrong, Deerslayer would pull on the rope. The empty canoe would then be out of reach of the Mingos.

Deerslayer waited an hour or so in the darkness. He couldn't even see where Tom and Harry had beached the other canoe. It was hidden in the dark, among the bushes.

Suddenly, the quiet night was broken by screams and cries. Deerslayer heard a dozen shots. He knew what had happened. More than four shots meant there were other guns at the Mingo camp. And other guns meant warriors. Harry and Old Tom had walked into a Mingo trap!

Quickly and quietly, Deerslayer pulled on the rope connected to the canoe on shore. He felt the canoe break loose of the shore, and he began to paddle hard for the ark. But what was wrong? Why was the light canoe so hard to pull? In an instant, he knew the answer. There was a Mingo hiding in the other canoe.

Without making any quick changes in his course, Deerslayer paddled away from the ark, and back toward the shore, far away from the Mingo camp. Deerslayer beached the canoe and quickly picked up his rifle. He knew that once the Mingo was on shore, the brave would come looking for him.

Deerslayer got ready. His moment of truth had come. He had never killed a man. But he knew that when the Mingo found him, he would have to kill or be killed. His keen ears heard sounds in the woods nearby. Then the bushes parted, and into the pale moonlight stepped a fierce Mingo brave!

"What do you want?" asked Deerslayer, his rifle aimed.

"Why do you try to steal my canoe?" asked the Mingo.

"I steal nothing," said Deerslayer, eyeing the rifle the Mingo held. "The canoe is mine. You have made a mistake."

"I found that canoe on the shore," persisted the Mingo.

"Yes, and with my rope tied to it," answered Deerslayer.

"I wondered about the rope," said the Mingo. "But Le Loup Cervier takes what he finds."

"And you are Le Loup Cervier?" asked Deerslayer.

"That I am. And a great warrior of the Mingo tribe."

"Then hear me well, Le Loup Cervier," said Deerslayer. "I have no wish to kill you, nor any man. I will take my canoe and go in peace."

A sly smile came over Le Loup Cervier's face. "I can be a man of peace, too," he said. "Take your boats and go."

Deerslayer breathed easier. He had not had to kill. He turned and walked toward his canoe. As he did, he heard a *click*. There was no mistaking the sound. The Mingo was pulling back the hammer on his rifle. He was going to shoot Deerslayer in the back!

In a flash, Deerslayer spun around and fired. The Mingo fell to the ground, a terrible wound in his chest. Deerslayer ran quickly to the fallen man.

The Mingo looked up at the white man. "Very well, take my scalp," he said bravely. "You have fought well. I don't fear you." He put his head back, as if offering his scalp to Deerslayer.

The white man put his rifle to one side. He knelt down and put the fallen brave into a comfortable position. "I do not take scalps," he told the Mingo. "I do not believe a white man should do such things."

The eyes of Le Loup Cervier grew wide. "You are like no white man I have ever met," he said. Then pain twisted the brave's face. "I am dying, white man," he said. "You have made a great *coup*. Le

Loup Cervier is a famous warrior. Before I die, I want to know your name."

"I am called two names," Deerslayer said softly. "Straight-tongue and Deerslayer."

"Those are good names," said Le Loup Cervier. "For I see you do not lie. And you shoot straight and true, even in the moonlight. But Deerslayer is no name for a warrior who could kill Le Loup Cervier. If I am still alive when my brothers find me, I shall call you by a proper name. To the Mingo, you will be known as Hawkeye."

"You do me honor," said Deerslayer. He stopped and listened. "I hear others coming," he said. "They have heard the shot. I must go, Le Loup Cervier."

"Then go," said Le Loup Cervier. "We will perhaps meet in the next world. For I know I am dying."

Deerslayer ran to his canoe. He turned back and looked at the Mingo on the bank. "Farewell, Le Loup Cervier," he called softly.

"Farewell, Hawkeye," called Le Loup Cervier.

4 Chingachgook Brings News

It was morning when Deerslayer caught sight of the ark. The currents of the lake had carried it far during the night. He also noticed that the ark was quite close to shore. This was dangerous, as the Mingos might be able to leap onto the flatboat from overhanging trees. Why hadn't the Hutter women poled the ark away from shore? Perhaps they were still asleep, Deerslayer thought.

As Deerslayer drew closer, gunfire broke out on shore. A moment later, a red man broke out of the woods, running hard. Behind him came a party of Mingos, firing as they ran. Deerslayer knew the first red man immediately. It was his old friend, Chingachgook, Chief of the Mohicans.

"Chingachgook!" cried Deerslayer. "Make for the flatboat. We have friends there!"

The firing had wakened Judith and Hetty Hutter. Judith appeared on deck and grabbed a pole. Deerslayer groaned to himself. If Judith moved the ark out too far, Chingachgook could not get on. Though Chingachgook was still a hundred yards away, Deerslayer called out.

"Judith! That red man is our friend. Let him on board!"

Judith Hutter turned, and she appeared to understand. At that very moment, Chingachgook gave a great jump and landed on the deck of the ark. Right behind him came two Mingos. Bracing himself as best he could, Deerslayer aimed and fired. One of the Mingos fell short, into the lake. The other landed on the ark!

Chingachgook turned and faced the Mingo. The combat didn't last long. In seconds, the Mingo tumbled overboard, wounded by Chingachgook. Judith and Hetty both grabbed poles, and aided by Chingachgook, they soon had the ark safely out on Glimmerglass. The rifle shots of the Mingos on shore could not reach them.

"Chingachgook!" cried Deerslayer, as he jumped on board. "How good to see you!"

"And it is good to see you, my brother," replied the red man. "For a time, I thought my death had come—at the hands of the Mingos."

"It'd take more than a Mingo party to kill you, old friend," said Deerslayer with a smile. "But I forget my manners. Chingachgook, this is Judith Hutter, and this is her sister, Hetty Hutter. Their father owns this boat . . . and forgive me, Judith and Hetty . . . I fear he is dead."

Judith's hands flew to her mouth, and Hetty gave a wild cry of despair. "Is it true, Natty?" asked Hetty.

"I fear so," said Deerslayer. "The campfires were a Mingo trap. I have little hope for your father and Harry."

"Wait, Deerslayer," said Chingachgook. "These men you speak of . . . Is one old, and the other a giant of a man?"

"Yes. What do you know about them?" asked Deerslayer.

"You needn't have any fear for their lives," said Chingachgook. "They still live. And if the Mingos didn't kill them right away, they have a reason. Maybe they want to deal with you for their release. Mingos will take ransom. But I don't trust their deals. They lie." Chingachgook almost spit out the

last words. He was as truthful as Deerslayer, and
both men had no respect for liars.

"Good news," said Deerslayer. "But how will we
know what the Mingos want in trade for Tom and
Harry?"

"Have no doubt that they will let you know,"
said Chingachgook. "They will send someone or
leave a sign. All we must do is wait."

"So we shall," said Deerslayer, with a smile. "And
while we wait, let us speak of our mission. Do you
have word of Hist?"

"Yes, I do. She is still with the Mingo war party.
Yocommon, the traitor, travels with her. Somewhere in those woods is my poor wife."

"You mean you two are just going to sit here and talk, and do nothing?" demanded Judith Hutter.

"I'm afraid there is little we can do but wait," said Deerslayer.

"Harry March wouldn't wait," said Judith.

"Harry March is a captive because he is a hot-head," pointed out Deerslayer. "I will not make that mistake."

While Chingachgook and Deerslayer were talking, no one noticed Hetty Hutter slip away. It wasn't until Deerslayer glanced at the shore that he saw her. Hetty had taken one of the canoes!

"Hetty, come back!" Deerslayer cried.

"I must help my father," the girl called back.

"Is the woman mad?" asked Chingachgook, in the language of his tribe. In the same language, Deerslayer explained to Chingachgook about Hetty.

Then he began to get a canoe so he could pursue Hetty, but Chingachgook stopped him. "It will do no good, Deerslayer," said Chingachgook. "You cannot catch her now. And the woods are alive with Mingos. You would lose your life or be captured yourself. Then, how could you help to get Hist back?"

As if to prove his point, Hetty was surrounded by Mingos as soon as she arrived at the shore. "For God's sake, Deerslayer," cried Judith, "take your rifle. Kill her, if you can. Or she will be taken by the Mingos. Then who knows what terrible things they will do to her?"

"The shot is too far," said Deerslayer. "And I do not believe they will harm her."

"Are you mad?" cried Judith. "She is a white woman, among savages!"

"If you'll forgive me," said Chingachgook, "to most of us red men, it is the white man who is a savage. He kills, but not for honor. He kills for money, taking scalps from babies and women. He lies and breaks his treaties. Your sister is safe, even among the treacherous Mingos."

"How can that be?" asked Judith.

"Because she is not right in the head," put in Deerslayer. "Mingos feel that people who are not right in the head are touched by God."

"As do we Mohicans," added Chingachgook.

"I pray you are right," said Judith.

"So do I," thought Deerslayer. But he said nothing aloud.

5 The Ransom

"But what can we use to ransom my father and Harry?" Judith asked Deerslayer. "We have nothing of value, except . . ." She paused.

"Anything might help," Deerslayer said. "There's no telling. Sometimes simple things will amuse people who have never seen them before. Think of a beautiful woman like yourself who's never seen a mirror. Many Indians never did, before the white man came."

"Then maybe we *do* have something on the ark. My father's treasure chest, as he calls it."

"What is inside?" asked Chingachgook.

"I don't know," Judith said. "Father hides the key to it. The lock is as strong as the chest itself. Come and see. It's in the ark's cabin."

"You're right," said Deerslayer, looking at the heavy chest. "I could try shooting off the lock, but the truth is that we can't waste the gunpowder. We may soon need it. Are you sure the key is on board?"

"Quite sure," said Judith. "He always hides it somewhere."

"Let me think, then," said Deerslayer. He sat down and was silent for a time. Finally, his face lit

up. "Miss Judith," he asked, "where are Hetty's things?"

"In her part of the cabin," she replied. "Over there."

Deerslayer began looking through Hetty's clothes. Unlike Judith's, they were plain. There was a Bible, but there was no jewelry or any other fancy items. In an apron pocket, Deerslayer found the key.

"That's amazing!" cried Judith. "How did you know the key would be there?"

"I thought of how Old Tom would think," said Deerslayer. "He wouldn't trust your curiosity, Miss Judith. Forgive me, but it's true. So he hid the key where someone not interested could find it and not care what the key fit. Miss Hetty, not being interested in the real world, was a natural choice. And here is the key. Now, I think we should leave, so you may open the trunk in private. What Old Tom has in there is not for outsiders to see."

Chingachgook and Deerslayer waited on deck for a few minutes. Then Judith came out. She was wearing a beautiful dress, one that she could have worn in the city. Out here, on Glimmerglass, Judith looked as if she could have come from another world.

"This, then, is Old Tom's secret treasure?" asked Chingachgook. "It will not buy much from the Mingos. They have seen white women's fancy dresses before."

"Oh, the treasure?" said Judith. "I saw this beautiful dress and had to try it on. But there wasn't much else in the chest. No gold or jewels. But there were a lot of papers and a chess set."

"A what?" asked Deerslayer.

"A chess set. Chess is a game played with small carved figures on a board. I'll show you." She went inside, and then quickly returned with two chess pieces. They were rooks carved from ivory, in the shape of elephants.

"You were wrong about there being no treasure," said Chingachgook. "These are beautiful carvings. I know nothing of the game you mention . . ."

"Chess," Judith said.

"Whatever its name," Chingachgook continued. "But animal carvings are thought by the Mingos to contain great magic. And I have never seen such an animal as this."

"It is an elephant," Judith said. "I have read about them, in books."

"I confess I haven't," said Deerslayer. "What little reading I have done has been the Bible. How big is this animal?"

When Judith told Deerslayer the size of an elephant, his eyes grew wide. He said no more, but it was plain he thought that perhaps Hetty wasn't the only Hutter sister who was not right in the head.

His thoughts were interrupted by noises from on shore. "Quick, Chingachgook!" he cried. "Mingos on shore. Get inside the cabin. If they see you, they will know of our mission!"

Chingachgook hid himself, as Deerslayer went to the side of the ark and looked toward the shore. He couldn't believe his eyes. Two Mingo warriors stood in the clearing. Between them, without so much as a scratch on her, was Hetty Hutter!

"What do you want?" cried Deerslayer to the Mingos.

"We have the two white cowards who tried to kill our women and children," called one warrior. "They did no damage. We were too smart for them. Then this mad woman came to us. She spoke to our chief of her God. She said that to kill the two white cowards would offend her God."

"And what did your chief say to this?" asked Deerslayer.

"He said that if these white men worshipped the same God she spoke of, they were poor worshippers. But our chief does not wish to offend any god. We will let the two white men go . . . for a price."

"What do you want for them?" asked Deerslayer.

"What do you offer?" asked the Mingo.

Deerslayer tossed one of the ivory elephants to the Mingo. The warrior looked it over, wonder

written on his face. He asked Deerslayer what animal this might be. Though he didn't believe a word, Deerslayer told the Mingo what Judith had told him of elephants. Then, he threw the other figure to the second Mingo on the shore.

"I will give you one ivory beast for each man," Deerslayer said, "if that is all right with your chief."

"You will have your answer soon," said the Mingo. The two Indians disappeared into the forest, leaving Hetty on the shore.

In hours, Old Tom and Hurry Harry were released. As soon as they were on board the ark, they poled off toward the log castle. There was great joy when Hetty and Judith were again with their father. Deerslayer introduced Chingachgook to the two men. True to form, they spoke with Chingachgook politely. But it was plain what they thought of him and all Indians.

"Well, what is next for you, Old Tom?" asked Deerslayer.

"First to the castle," said Tom. "I have two old pistols there. The Mingos let us go, but they kept our rifles."

"Have you a need of these things right away?" asked Deerslayer. "Surely you can wait. Buy others when the British army patrols come through. From what Harry told me, they should be here any day now."

"You don't understand, lad," said Harry. "We
have been inside the Mingo camp. We now know
how they guard it. This time, when we raid for
scalps, we won't get caught!"

Deerslayer shook his head in wonder. Harry and Tom hadn't learned a thing. All they could think of was scalp money. He would have spoken, but he knew better. He and Chingachgook needed these men and the ark. If Hist could be freed, the ark and the log castle would be the only safe places until the army patrol arrived.

Still marveling at the greed and ignorance of the two men, Deerslayer helped pole the ark toward the log castle.

6 A Mingo Ambush

As the great flatboat glided toward the castle, Deerslayer and Chingachgook had time to speak with Hetty. Harry and Tom were busy with their plans for yet another raid on the Mingos.

"Tell me, Miss Hetty," asked Deerslayer, "when you were in the Mingo camp, did you meet any of their women?"

"None to speak with, save one," replied Hetty, "and she was not of their tribe."

"Tell us more of her," said Chingachgook excitedly. "What was her name?"

"She told me two names. Wah-ta!-wah, and the other—"

"Was it Hist?" asked Chingachgook.

"Yes, that was it!" cried Hetty. "And she also spoke of Deerslayer and Chingachgook. That would be you?"

"It is."

"She said she was stolen from her people and her husband. She said that in two days, she will try to escape and join Deerslayer. She didn't know you were here, Chingachgook."

"What did she say of escape?" asked Deerslayer.

"That she would be in the clearing near the lake at sunset, two days from now."

"Near the camp we saw?"

"No," said Hetty. "They are moving the camp to the other side of the lake, not far from the castle. That is where she will try to join you."

Chingachgook and Deerslayer spent the rest of the day making plans. They didn't speak with Tom and Harry, who were busy with plans of their own. As the sun was setting, the ark neared the great log castle.

"There she is, safe and sound," said Old Tom, as the flatboat came to rest alongside the castle. "Well, let's be getting inside."

"I would wait until clear daylight, if I were you," said Deerslayer.

"Why?" asked Harry. "It's plain there's no one inside. The Mingos are on the other side of the lake."

"I wouldn't be too sure," said Chingachgook.

"They don't want us anymore," said Old Tom. "They have their toy elephants to play with."

"Don't make that mistake," said Chingachgook. "The Mingos made a deal for you. But that doesn't mean they still won't kill you, if they get the chance. Killing a prisoner is different from man-to-man fighting. In fair combat, they would offend no god."

"Ahh, you worry too much," said Harry, jumping to the shore. Tom followed him. "Coming along, you two?" called Harry.

"We will stay here, in case anything goes wrong," said Deerslayer.

"Suit yourself," said Harry, and the two men went inside.

In seconds, a shot rang out. There were screams and cries. Deerslayer heard Harry cry out, "A trap! Get the women and the boat clear!"

Chingachgook and Deerslayer needed no further word. They poled the ark to safety. A Mingo appeared at the doorway of the castle, facing the lake. Deerslayer fired, and the man fell. There were more cries from inside.

Suddenly, Harry appeared at the top of the tower of the log castle. He was locked in a life-and-death struggle with two Mingo warriors. As Chingachgook poled the ark, Deerslayer threw a long rope into the water. "Jump, Harry!" he called.

He might have been greedy and ignorant, but Harry March was a tiger in battle. Somehow, he freed himself from the grip of one Mingo. With a blow of his huge arm, he knocked the Mingo cold. A well-placed kick brought the other one low. Before either Mingo could recover, Harry dove off the tower and into Glimmerglass. Deerslayer and Chingachgook pulled him to safety.

"Well, what do you think now of the Mingo?" asked Deerslayer of Harry. "Still think they're simple children playing with their toys?"

"I must admit you were right," Harry said. "There were five Mingos in the castle, waiting for us. I killed one, I know. Another, I'm not sure."

"What of my father?" asked Hetty.

"I'm sorry," said the big man. "I saw what happened. I saw his wound. He's dead, Miss Hetty." Hetty let out a scream and then fell to the deck in a faint.

The ark lay off the lakeshore through the night. When the sun rose, Chingachgook and Deerslayer poled the boat close to the castle. They went ashore with Harry to see if any Mingos were in the area. There were no Mingos in sight, so Hetty and

Judith joined the men on the shore. They all went right to the castle and found Tom Hutter in a small room.

He was terrible to see. He had been scalped, and he lay quite still. Hetty and Judith rushed to his side. "He's bleeding so!" cried Hetty.

"What?" cried Deerslayer. "Dead men don't bleed. He's still alive!"

They made Hutter as comfortable as possible. Hetty brought him water. Tom's eyes flickered, and then they opened. He saw Judith and Hetty, and he smiled weakly.

"I never thought I'd see you again," he said, in a whisper.

"Don't talk. Save your strength," said Deerslayer.

"It doesn't matter now, lad," said Hutter. "I am dying and I know it. I must talk. I must tell Judith and Hetty." All fell silent as they listened to Tom Hutter's tale.

"You are not my true daughters," the old man said. "I love you as much . . . couldn't love you more. But the truth is that I met your mother when she already had two baby girls—yourselves. I haven't been a good man in my life. You two girls are the best thing that ever happened to me in all my sorry years. Please think well of me, if you can." With these words, Tom Hutter died.

The sad group got aboard the ark, carrying Tom Hutter's body. They poled the boat to where Judith and Hetty's mother had been buried, beneath the waters of Glimmerglass. And there, they laid Tom Hutter to rest.

"We must plan, Deerslayer," said Chingachgook. "Hist will be at the clearing near the castle in a day's time. And though I don't trust him, we must tell Harry of our mission."

"I agree," said Deerslayer. "And I don't trust him, either."

7 Deerslayer Keeps His Word

Without a sound, Chingachgook and Deerslayer beached the canoes near the castle. The sun was setting, but there was no sign of Hist in the clearing. Cautiously, they circled the area. Soon it was growing dark.

"I will wait in the clearing for her," Deerslayer whispered to Chingachgook. "She expects to see me. In the darkness, she might think you are a Mingo, by your clothing."

"I understand, Deerslayer," said Chingachgook, with a slight smile. "But I think Hist would know me, even if I were dressed like a white man."

They waited for what seemed like hours. By now a full moon was shining above the lake. Finally, there was a motion in the bushes. Into the clearing stepped one of the most beautiful red women one could ever wish to see.

"Deerslayer!" she called softly, rushing to the white man. "I fear for Chingachgook," she said. "I heard talk in the Mingo camp of a Mohican they were hunting—"

"Have no fear," said Chingachgook, as he stepped from the shadows. "I am safe, and I have come for you."

The two embraced, as Deerslayer looked discreetly in another direction. As he did, a sudden movement caught his eye. Hist had been followed! "Run, Chingachgook!" cried Deerslayer. "They are upon us!"

In a second, a party of ten Mingos rushed from the trees. Chingachgook sprang to Deerslayer's side, his tomahawk at the ready. Deerslayer fired at a charging Mingo. The man fell.

"Don't stay here, Chingachgook," cried Deerslayer. "Save Hist! I'll hold them off!"

"I obey, to save her," said Chingachgook. "But I shall return, if yet you live, my friend."

"Don't talk—run!" cried Deerslayer, as the Mingos rushed again.

Chingachgook and Hist made it safely to the canoes. The last they saw of Deerslayer, he was overrun by Mingos holding tomahawks. Safely out of range of Mingo fire, Chingachgook swung the canoe around. Deerslayer was on the ground, with several Mingos holding him down. Were they about to scalp him?

One of the Mingos walked to the edge of the lake and called out. "You, Mohican dog, and your woman. Do you hear me?"

"I hear you, Mingo."

"Know me, then, Mohican. I am Rivenoak, Chief of the Mingos."

"Whatever you call yourself, you are a coward and a woman stealer," called back Chingachgook. "I am Chingachgook, Chief of the Mohicans. What does a barking dog ask of a chief?"

"We have your friend, Hawkeye . . . or so he was called by the fallen Le Loup Cervier. He has fought bravely. We have no wish to take his scalp. He did not take that of Le Loup Cervier. But if you want the white man back, you will hear my terms."

"And what are these terms, Rivenoak?"

"I will make them known when I am ready. Farewell, Chingachgook, chief of running dogs." With these words, the Mingo chief motioned to the warriors. Tied hand and foot, Deerslayer was carried into the woods.

Sadly, Chingachgook and Hist returned to the ark. The news of Deerslayer's capture seemed to upset Judith more than anyone else. The lovely Hist spoke privately with her.

"Please don't fear for Deerslayer," Hist told Judith. "He is a great hunter and warrior. He knew that at any time he could lose his life in hunting or in battle. This is the way of the warrior. We red people understand this."

"It's what you *don't* understand," said Judith, tearfully. "I love him."

Hist frowned. "I have heard him say that his life is the forest. He said he'd ask no woman to share it."

"But I have lived in the forest, here on the ark, and in the castle," said Judith. "I know the way of the wild. I had hoped to prove this to him. Now he's a prisoner."

"Yet he lives," said Hist. "We may see his return."

"I pray so," said Judith.

Sometimes, in this world, prayers are answered. The people aboard the ark were amazed the next morning when a call from the shore woke them.

Standing alone and free in a small clearing was Deerslayer. He was quickly welcomed aboard.

"I thought they would kill you," said Harry March.

"It is not so easy for anyone to kill Deerslayer," said Chingachgook. "But what of the ransom, my brother?" he asked Natty.

"I am not free, as you think," Deerslayer replied. "After I spoke with Rivenoak, he told me his terms. And because I showed respect for the man I killed, Le Loup Cervier, they trusted me. They have let me come here to tell you what the Mingos demand."

"Demand?" cried Harry. "We are here on the ark, safe. We have guns. The British army will be here soon. All we have to do is stay alive until they come. Forget the Mingos and their terms. They'll soon have lead shot for *our* terms."

Deerslayer smiled sadly. "You don't understand, Hurry Harry. Neither me, nor the life I live. I have given my word to the Mingos that I'll return."

"What's a word to a redskin?" Harry said. "The Mingos broke promises; they lied. They even stole your friend's wife. You don't have to keep your word to a Mingo!"

"It is *my* word that has been given, Harry," said Deerslayer. "And if I had given my word to the Devil himself, I would still honor it."

"I understand, brother," said Chingachgook. "But what are Rivenoak's terms?"

"Simply these," said Deerslayer. "Chingachgook may go in peace. My life will be spared, as will yours, Harry. But Hetty, Judith, and Hist must remain with the Mingos, as Mingo women."

"Never!" cried Hurry Harry.

"Then I must return," Deerslayer said. "But this doesn't mean we can't plan."

"What do you have in mind?" Chingachgook asked.

"First, I think Harry should slip away tonight, in the darkness. The soldiers can't be far away."

"And then?" asked Chingachgook.

"You, Hist, and the Hutter women will stay on the raft, until the army arrives."

"And you?" asked Judith.

"I must return," said Deerslayer.

"I must speak with you, alone," said Judith. "I have something to show you. It is in my father's treasure chest."

"Very well, Miss Judith," said Deerslayer, following her into the ark's cabin.

Making sure they were not heard by the others, Judith turned to Deerslayer. "You can't go back, Natty," she cried. "Stay. We can all live. And you must know I love you. I have never spoken these words to any man. I can be your wife, Natty. I can be a good wife."

Deerslayer shook his head sadly. "Miss Judith, you're a fine woman. But no woman . . . not even

a red woman . . . could share my life. I am what I am. One day, you would long for the life in the towns. You would want to wear fine clothing. You would long for the company of other whites. I have no such needs. And what I have seen of men like Harry proves that. Now I must rejoin the others. We must make further plans." He walked toward the door to the cabin.

"But I love you. I want you!" cried Judith.

Deerslayer turned. "In this life, we get so little of what we want," he said. Then he went out on deck.

During the night, Hurry Harry slipped away. As Chingachgook and Deerslayer watched him disappear into the darkness, the red man said, "What do you think his chances are?"

"He knows the forest well for a white man," Deerslayer said. "And the British are nearby, someplace." He smiled sadly. "And just now, I'd say his chances are a lot better than mine!"

8 Under Sentence of Death

The Mingo sentry turned in amazement. Standing behind him was Deerslayer. He had heard no sound as the white man approached. The Mingo lowered his half-raised tomahawk. "You move like smoke in the forest, Hawkeye," the sentry said, calling Deerslayer by his Mingo name.

"No, sentry," said Deerslayer. "I move like a Mohican."

The sentry spit on the ground. "The Mohicans are old women, afraid of a fight."

"That may be," said Deerslayer, "yet the Mingo have counted their dead in war with the Mohicans in the past. But enough of this. I must speak with Rivenoak. Pass me through safely."

The Mingo sentry cupped his hands to his mouth and gave a cry. A white man would have taken it for the call of a bird. But in seconds, an answering call came, from deeper in the forest. "They know you are coming, Hawkeye," said the sentry. Another, different birdcall came from the forest. "They want to know if you are alone."

"I have not brought the women, as you can see," said Deerslayer.

The sentry gave another birdcall, and then he turned to Deerslayer. "You know that you go to your death, Hawkeye?"

Deerslayer shrugged. "We shall all meet death, one day, won't we, sentry?" he said. "I hope I go to mine with honor."

"You are a brave man, Hawkeye," the sentry said. "May the Great Spirit make you strong in death."

"Thank you, sentry," said Deerslayer, and he walked to the Mingo camp.

As he entered the camp, Deerslayer was ringed by crowds of Mingo warriors and women. Small boys threw stones and jeered. Then Rivenoak stepped from his tent and stopped the crowd with a wave of his hand.

"You have returned, Hawkeye," he said. "You surprise me. When shall the women be given to us? "

"You make a mistake, Rivenoak," Deerslayer said. "The others will not agree to your terms."

The Mingo's eyes widened. "Yet you come back here? You know you face torture and death? We Mingos are not gentle with prisoners, as you know." He moved his hand toward his belt. A new, still-bloody scalp hung from it . . . Tom Hutter's.

"I am known as Deerslayer and Straight-tongue, among the Mohicans. I have given my word. I have returned," Deerslayer said.

Rivenoak raised his hands to the crowd of Mingos. "Hawkeye has kept his word," he said. "The torture will begin, unless one Mingo speaks in his favor." His eyes scanned the crowd. "Does anyone speak for Hawkeye?"

There was a long silence. The crowd pressed closer to Deerslayer. Hands reached out, ready to strike the first blow. Then a woman's voice called out.

"I speak out for Hawkeye!"

"Who speaks?" asked Rivenoak.

"I, Le Sumac," said a Mingo woman, stepping out of the crowd.

"You are the widow of Le Loup Cervier," said Rivenoak. "This man has killed your husband. Yet you speak for his life. Why?"

"I wish only what is fair," said Le Sumac. She was a handsome red woman, just in her twenties, and as she came forward, she stood next to Deerslayer. "I have a son to be fed," she said. "Now he has no father to teach him the ways of the forest. It is true Hawkeye has slain Le Loup Cervier. But like no other white man, he fought with honor. He did not take Le Loup Cervier's scalp. Because of this, my husband has entered the other world whole in body and spirit.

"Yet still my lodge is empty. This man is a great hunter and warrior. I say spare his life, if he will be my husband and raise my son to be brave and wise as he."

"What you say makes sense, Le Sumac," said Rivenoak. He turned to Deerslayer. "What do you say to this, Hawkeye? Will you become a Mingo? Will you be husband to Le Sumac, and father to Le Loup Cervier's son? Speak!"

Deerslayer was silent for a time. Then, slowly, he spoke. "I honor the widow of Le Loup Cervier," he said, "as I honor the bravery of her husband. I feel sorrow that her son has no father. Could I undo Le Loup Cervier's death, I would. I take neither pleasure nor pride in killing. But if I had not killed Le Sumac's husband, he would have killed me. Such is the way of the warrior and hunter."

"You speak well and truthfully, Hawkeye," said Rivenoak. "But you have not answered Le Sumac. Will you be her husband?"

"You have praised me for giving my word and keeping it," Deerslayer said. "So must I honor my word. I am sworn a blood brother to Chingachgook, Chief of the Mohicans. Though Le Sumac is capable and beautiful, I cannot accept her offer.

"My life is in the forest. Although I visit the camps of the Mohican to bring food, I live in the forest. I need no tent. The sky is my roof. My lodge is the green woods. No woman, red or white, could live as I do. Not even the widow of a great Mingo warrior.

"But the most important reason of all is that I will not be a traitor to my blood brother. I am not like Yocommon."

A howl like the cry of a mad animal came from the crowd. Then a red man pushed his way to the front. It was Yocommon, the traitor. "I will show you how Yocommon can fight!" he cried. He

reached to his belt and grabbed his tomahawk. Then he sent it spinning with deadly force at Deerslayer!

Deerslayer didn't flinch. Without even changing his expression, the white man moved his hand faster than a striking snake. He plucked the tomahawk from the air, inches from his face. The crowd gasped in amazement. But this drove Yocommon to madness. "Die, Deerslayer!" he screamed, and drawing his knife, he rushed at the white man.

Deerslayer stood his ground, and again his right hand flashed in the air. The tomahawk buried itself deep into Yocommon's forehead. Yocommon fell in the dust, dead at Deerslayer's feet.

The crowd backed away as Yocommon's body was dragged to his lodge. Rivenoak scowled at Deerslayer. "Another man is dead at your hands, Hawkeye," said the chief. "True, he was a traitor to his own tribe. I did not trust him. Yet he had become a Mingo. For killing him, you must die."

"You saw that I was unarmed, Rivenoak," said Deerslayer. "I killed to avoid being killed. As I did with Le Loup Cervier."

"I have eyes, Hawkeye. I know. But the law of the Mingo is our law. It saddens me to see a great warrior like yourself die. Yet you refuse any reasonable offer."

Rivenoak turned to the crowd. "Let the torture begin!" he called. In a second, ten pairs of Mingo hands grabbed Deerslayer. He was quickly dragged to a post driven into the ground, and his hands and feet were tied behind him.

"Before you die, Hawkeye," said Rivenoak, "we will first test your courage." He nodded to a Mingo brave, who stood twenty feet away from the post to which Deerslayer was tied. The man stared at Deerslayer, and then he threw his tomahawk. The razor-sharp ax came spinning through the air, straight at Deerslayer's head!

9 The Rescue

The tomahawk landed an inch from Deerslayer's head and buried itself deep into the post to which he was tied. But if the Mingos had thought to see Deerslayer flinch, they were disappointed. Time after time, Mingo warriors sent axes and knives whistling at the white man's head and body. Deerslayer moved not one muscle.

"Enough!" called Rivenoak. "The man has shown his great courage. We will not make him suffer any longer. The next warrior to throw will strike true. I command that the next warrior be The Panther, brother of Le Sumac. So shall Le Loup Cervier's death be avenged."

A huge Mingo warrior took his place before the post that held Deerslayer fast. He drew his tomahawk, took slow aim, raised his arm . . .

"Stop!" cried a woman's voice. All heads turned. Into the camp, clad in the fancy dress from Tom Hutter's treasure chest, walked Judith Hutter! Behind her came her sister, Hetty.

"What is this all about?" demanded Rivenoak. "And who are you, white woman? I know the woman with you. She has been touched by God. But I have never seen you."

"As well you shouldn't," said Judith. "I am the daughter of a general in the British army. Even now, as we speak, they are marching toward this camp. The man you have here is to be my husband. If the man is harmed, the entire British army will make war on the Mingos."

Rivenoak looked at Judith, then to Deerslayer, in puzzlement. "Hawkeye, do you know this woman?" he asked.

"That I do," said Deerslayer, and he said no more.

"Yet you have turned down an offer for a Mingo wife. Have you lied, Hawkeye? I cannot tell. I know that you are brave. But did you lie, despite your Mohican name of Straight-tongue? How can I know whether to believe you or this white woman?"

Rivenoak glanced around him. Then his face brightened. "I know how to solve this," he said. "The other white woman is known to me. She does not have the wits to lie. And though her mind may not be right, she speaks only the truth." He turned to Hetty Hutter and asked, "Is this woman who she says she is? Is the British army going to make war on the Mingos?"

Hetty smiled sweetly and said, "That is my sister, Judith. Doesn't she look pretty in her new dress?"

"Seize the woman!" cried Rivenoak. "It was a trick!"

The Panther strode to Judith Hutter. He reached for her. As he did, a shot rang out. The Panther

fell dead. Then, with a fearful cry, a figure burst out of the woods, a tomahawk in one hand, a knife in the other. It was Chingachgook, warrior, and Chief of the Mohicans. His hand flashed, and his tomahawk struck deep into Rivenoak's shoulder.

Screams and cries filled the air. Suddenly more shots rang out. Chingachgook ran quickly to where Deerslayer was tied. In a heart's beat, he had cut the ropes binding the white man. "Who is with you?" asked Deerslayer.

"I don't know," said Chingachgook quickly. "I thought I was alone!"

The question was quickly answered. Into the camp burst Hurry Harry March, firing as he came. Behind him, in bright red coats, came a platoon of British soldiers. Soon gunsmoke was as thick in the air as the cries of the wounded and dying.

The Mingos scattered like leaves before a strong wind. By the time the smoke had cleared, the camp was deserted, except for the dead and wounded on the ground.

Judith Hutter raced to Deerslayer's side. "Are you all right, Natty?" she cried.

"I live," said Deerslayer. "Are you unharmed?"

"Yes, I am fine," she said. Then she looked around her. Her eyes fastened on a fallen figure. "Good Lord!" she screamed. "It's Hetty. She's hurt!"

They rushed to the fallen woman. Deerslayer gathered Hetty up in his arms. He carried her to a

grassy spot, below a tree, and gently set her down.
There was a terrible wound in Hetty's chest. Her
breath came in slow gasps.

"Hetty, can you hear me?" asked Deerslayer,
softly. Hetty's eyes opened.

"Natty," she said, with a weak smile. "It hurts so!"

"Yes, it must," Deerslayer said, his eyes avoiding
the wound that was slowly taking away Hetty's life.

"You are a good man, Natty," Hetty said. "And I
love you. So does Judith." She gasped in sudden
pain. Then, like a great weight being lifted, her
spirit left her body. Deerslayer closed the poor
girl's still-opened eyes.

Hetty Hutter was buried in Glimmerglass, near her mother and her stepfather, Tom Hutter. On the following day, leaving Judith in the care of Hurry Harry and the British, Deerslayer said his farewells.

"Will I never see you again, Natty?" asked Judith.

"Never is a long time," said Deerslayer. "If God wills, we may meet again, Miss Judith."

Then, with a wave, Deerslayer, Chingachgook, and Hist disappeared into the forest that would always be home to Natty Bumppo: Deerslayer to the Mohicans . . . Hawkeye to the Mingos.